A Mark Portfolio

The Boy Who Loved Monopoly

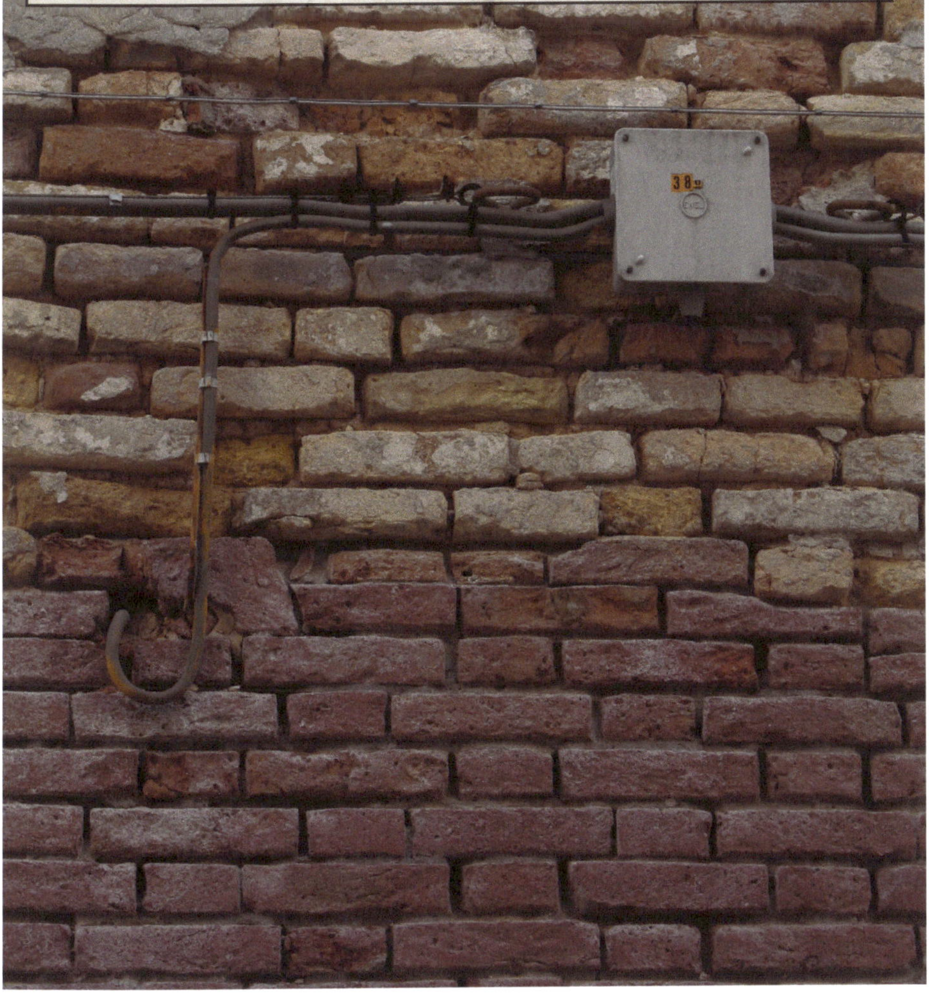

Mark Dahle Portfolios can be read in a few minutes
and enjoyed for a lifetime.

Unlike many picture books, the text is not related to the
photographs and painting. This might seem a little weird at first.
One thing that makes it better is to order more portfolios until
you get used to it. In the meantime, space is provided on the
pages for you to draw your own pictures if you like.

This portfolio includes a story about a boy who loved playing the
board game Monopoly, a photo of a great 36 x 24 inch abstract
painting (at the right) and twenty-seven beautiful photos of
Venice, Italy.

Photographs in this book are available in limited editions.
See http://www.MarkDahle.com for more information
and for previews of upcoming portfolios.

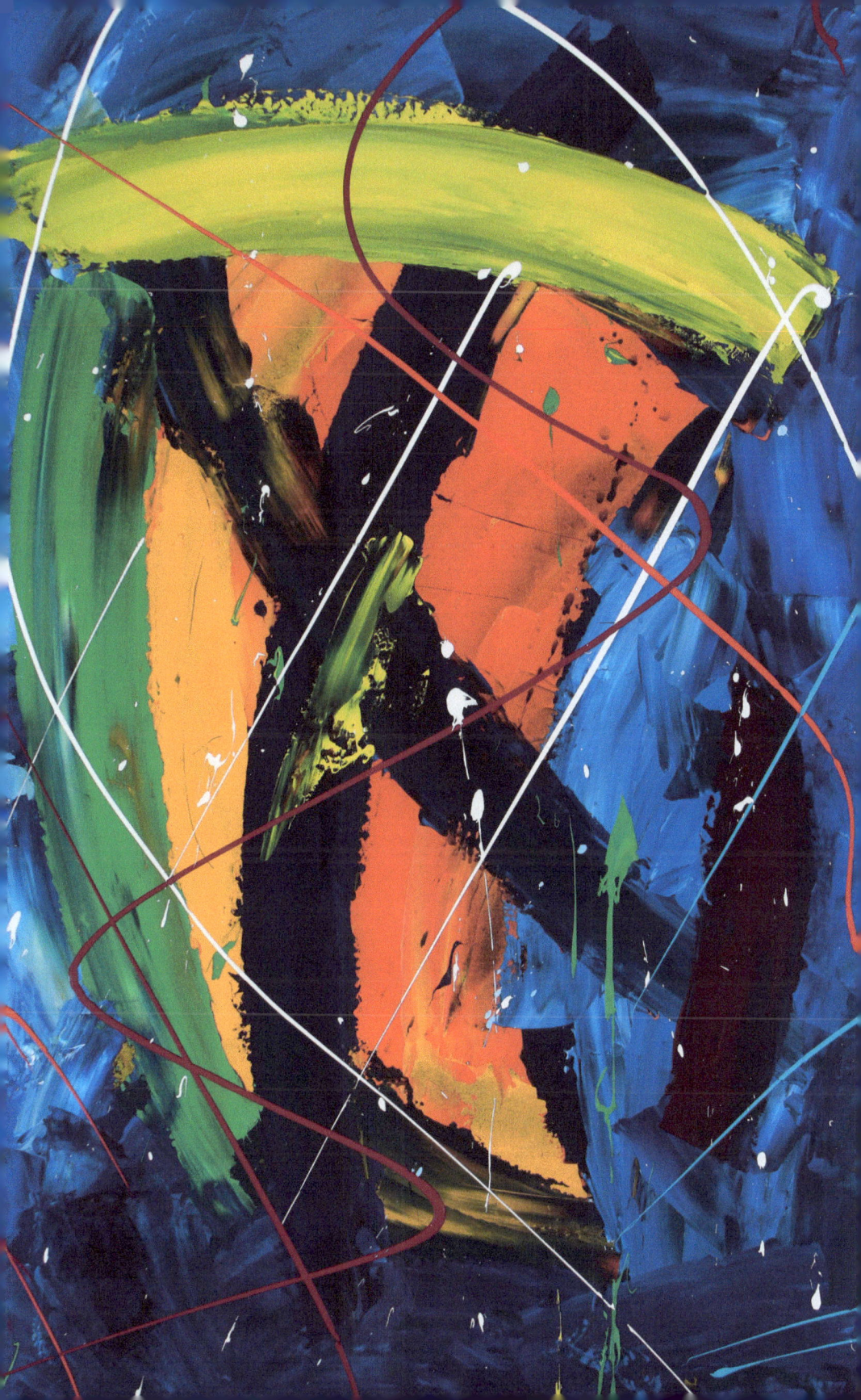

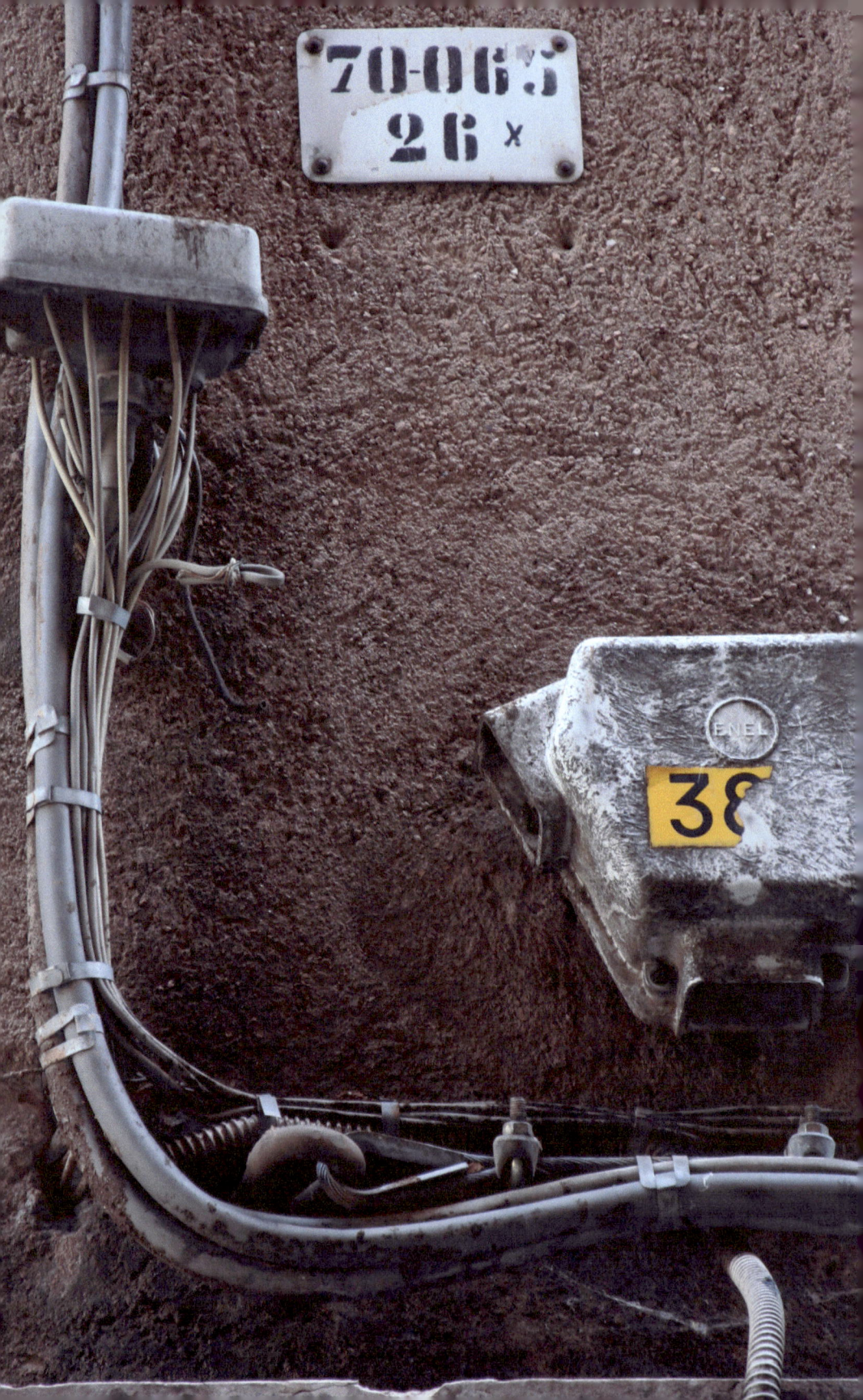

Once there was a boy
who loved to play
Monopoly.

He was not very good at it,
so he did not win very often.

But he loved to play the game.

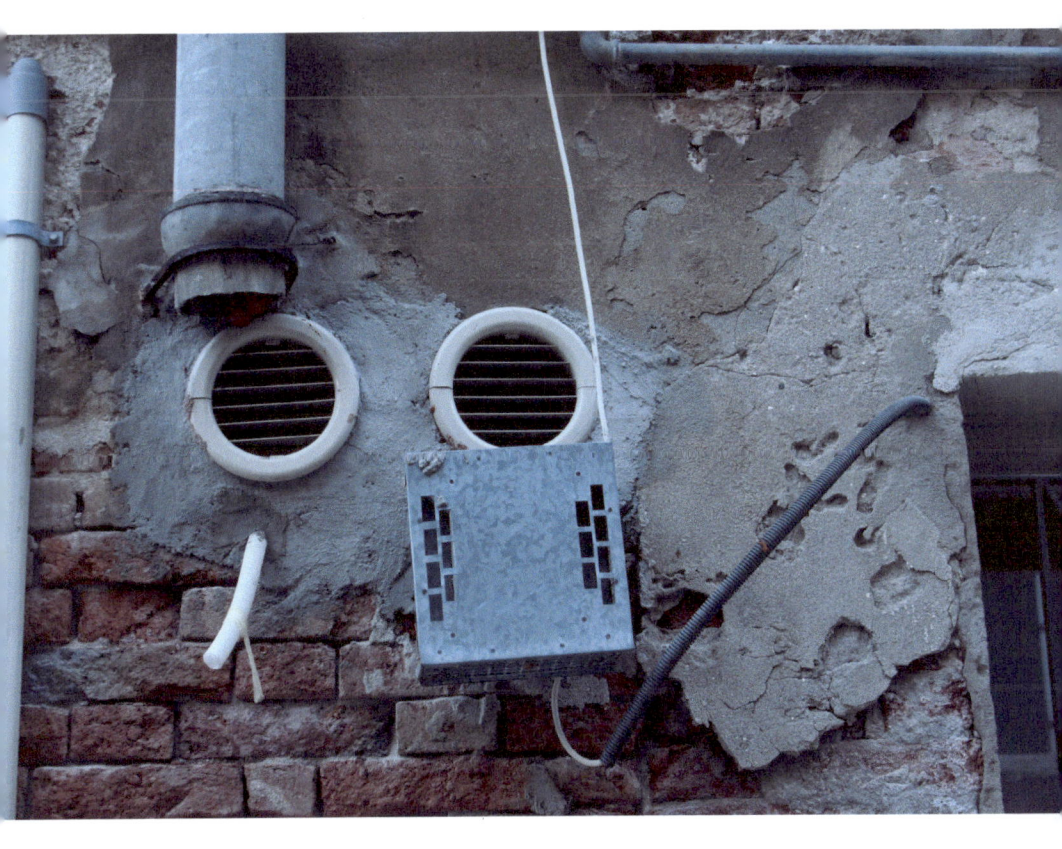

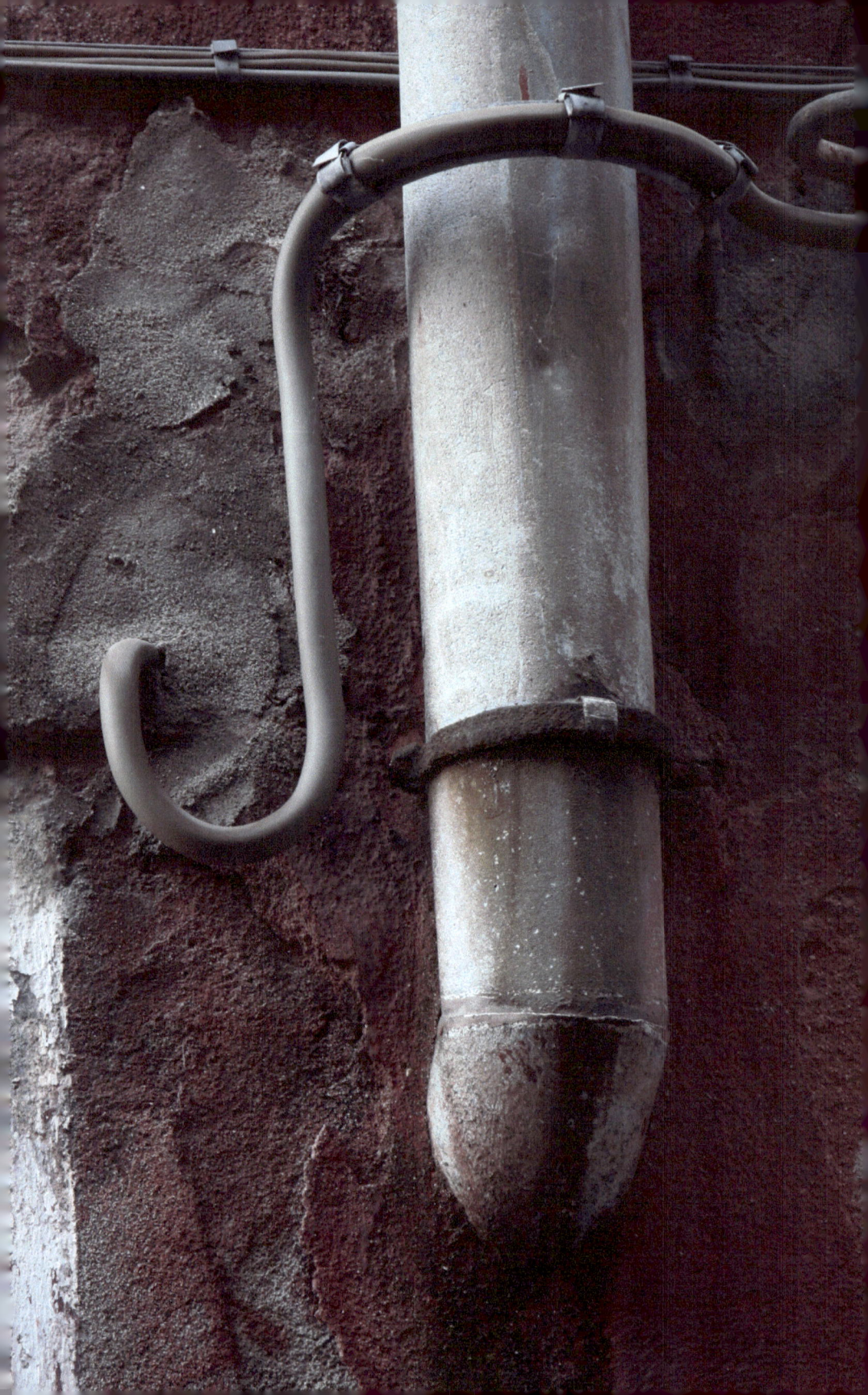

He played with his three friends
every chance he got.

When they weren't around,
he played solitaire Monopoly.

And, once in a while,
he even played with his younger sister,
who never followed the rules.

That's how much
he loved to play Monopoly!

It was his favorite thing to do.

One day
the boy received a check
for $250,000
as an inheritance.

The boy took the check to the bank.

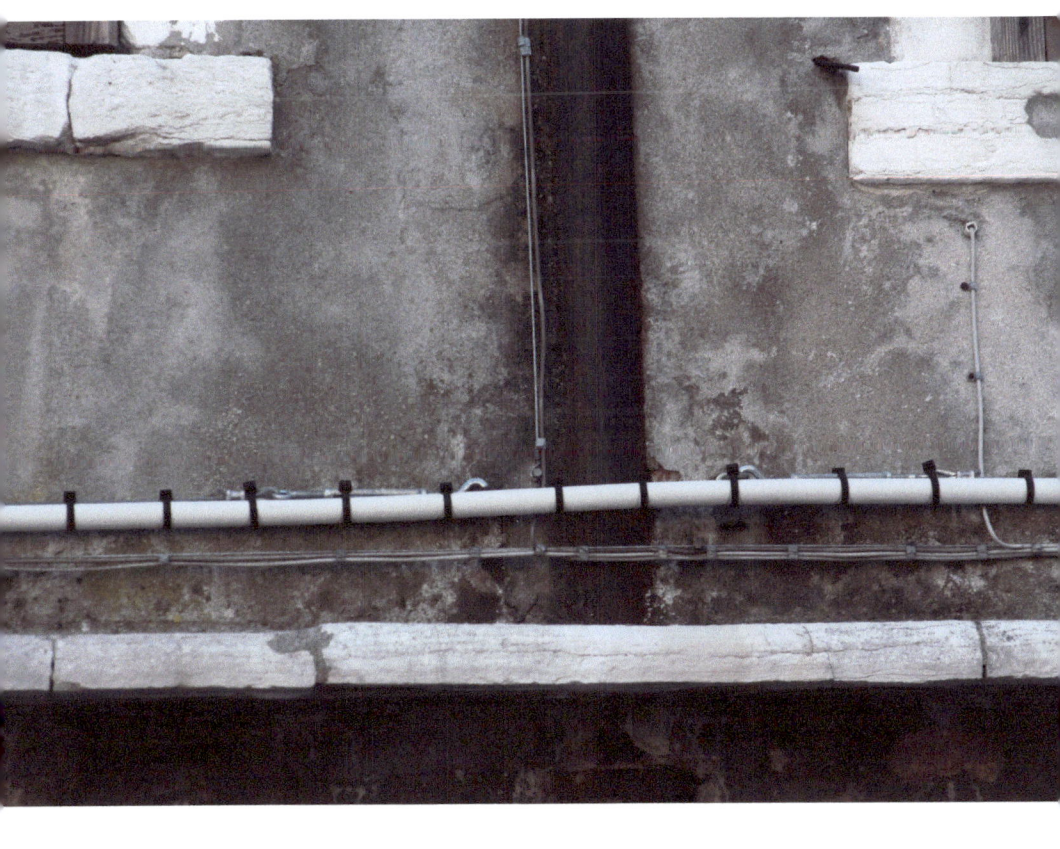

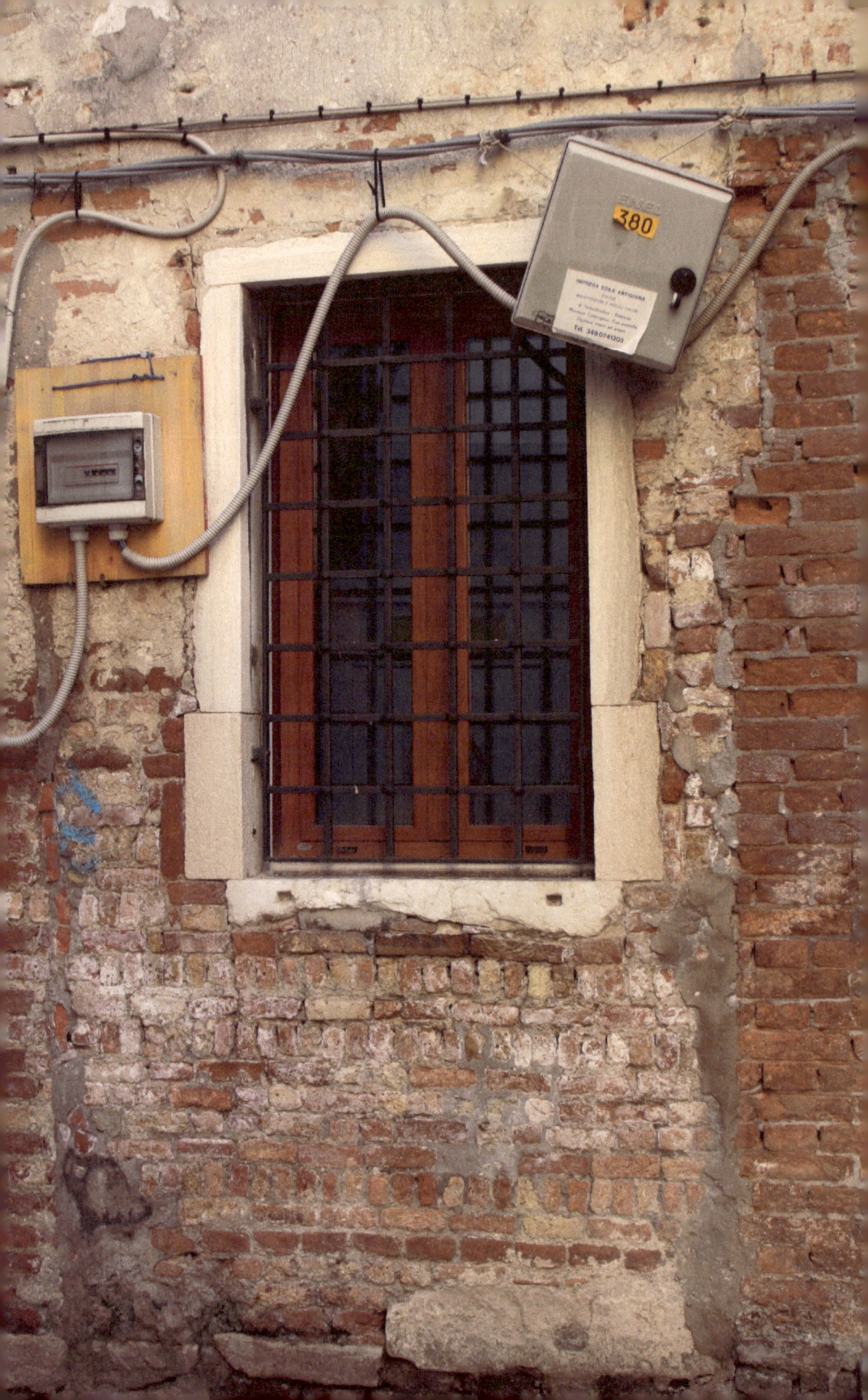

The teller gave the boy some $1 bills.
She gave him some $5 bills.
She gave him some $10 bills.
She gave him some $20 bills.
She gave him some $50 bills.
And she gave him quite a few $100 bills.

What would he do
with his fortune?

What would *you* do?

Well, the boy loved to play Monopoly.
And he rarely won.
But now he had money.

The next time he played
at his friends' house,
he brought some of his money
to the game.

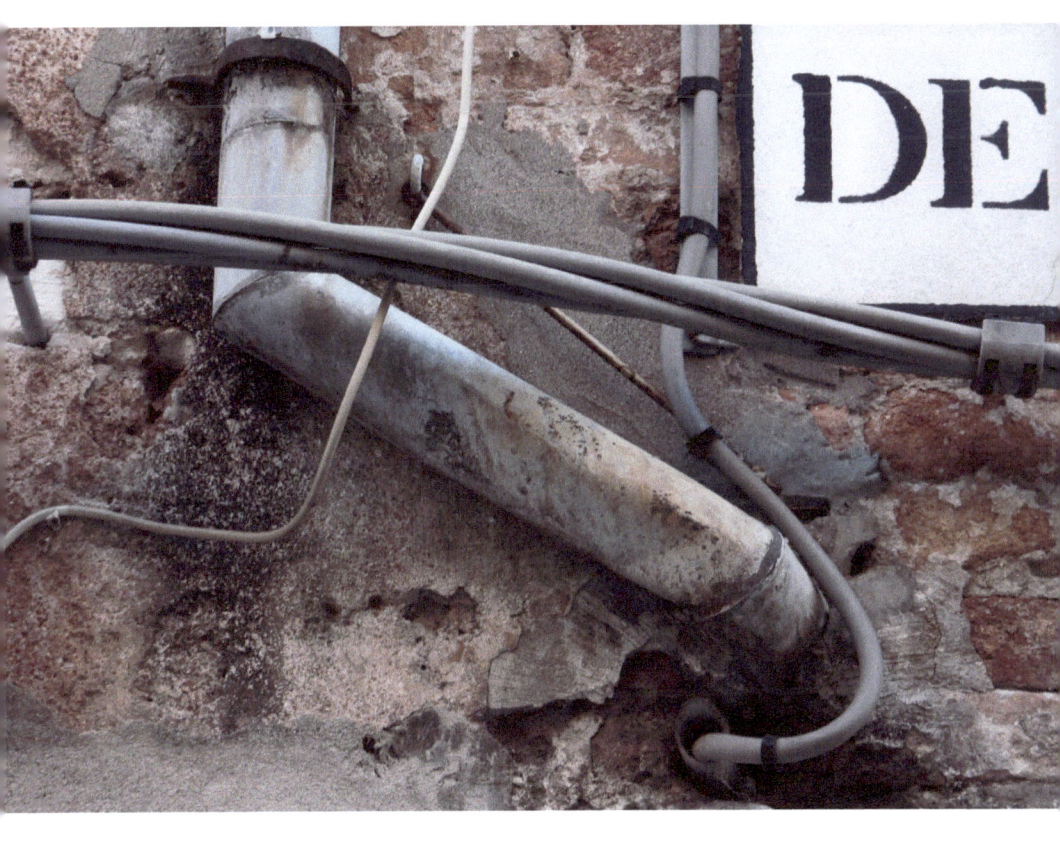

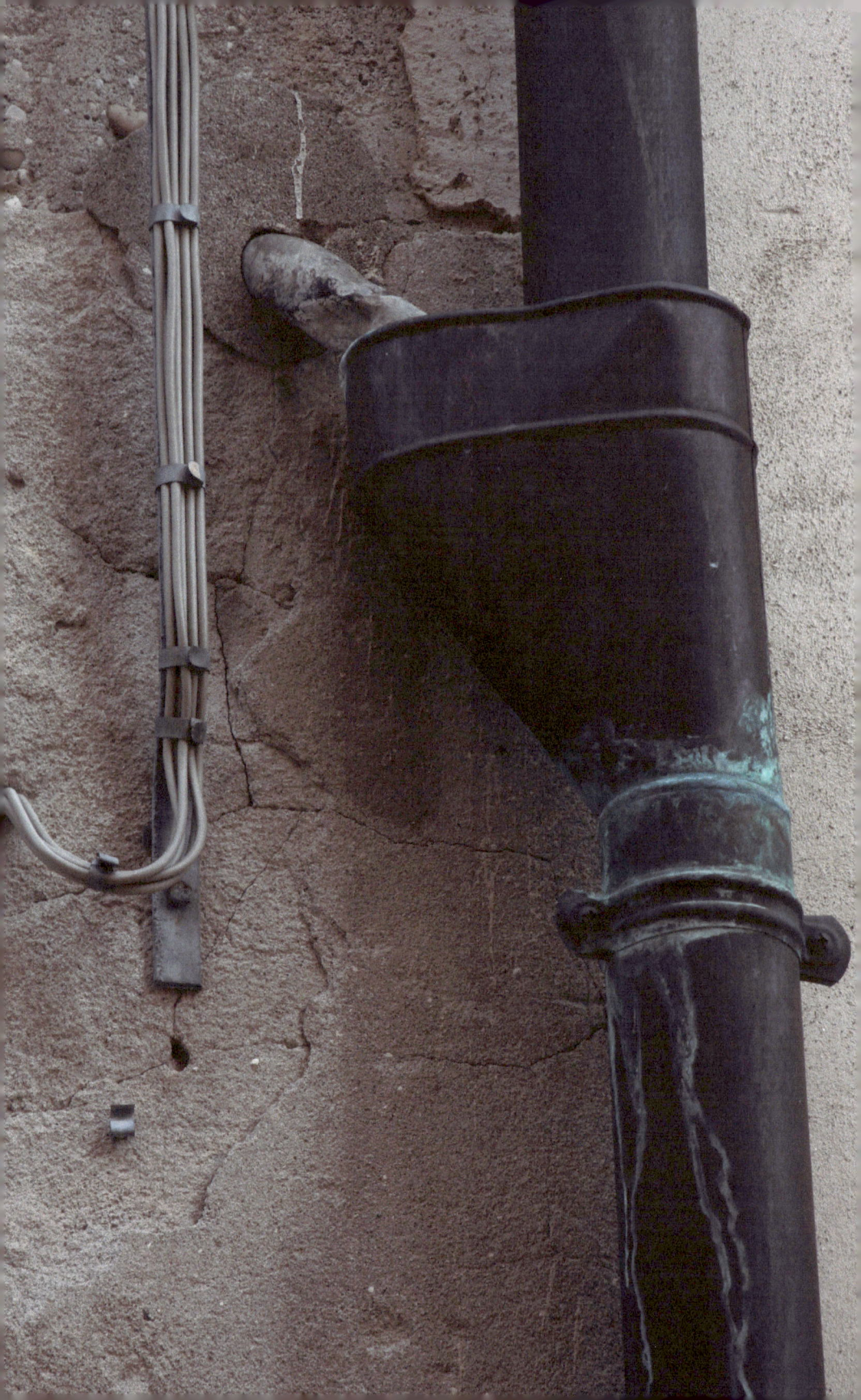

When everyone else
got their money from the banker,
he got the same amount.

All the players
got five $1 bills
and five $5 bills.

All the players
got five $10 bills
and six $20 bills.

All the players
got two $50 bills
and two $100 bills.

All the players
got two $500 bills.

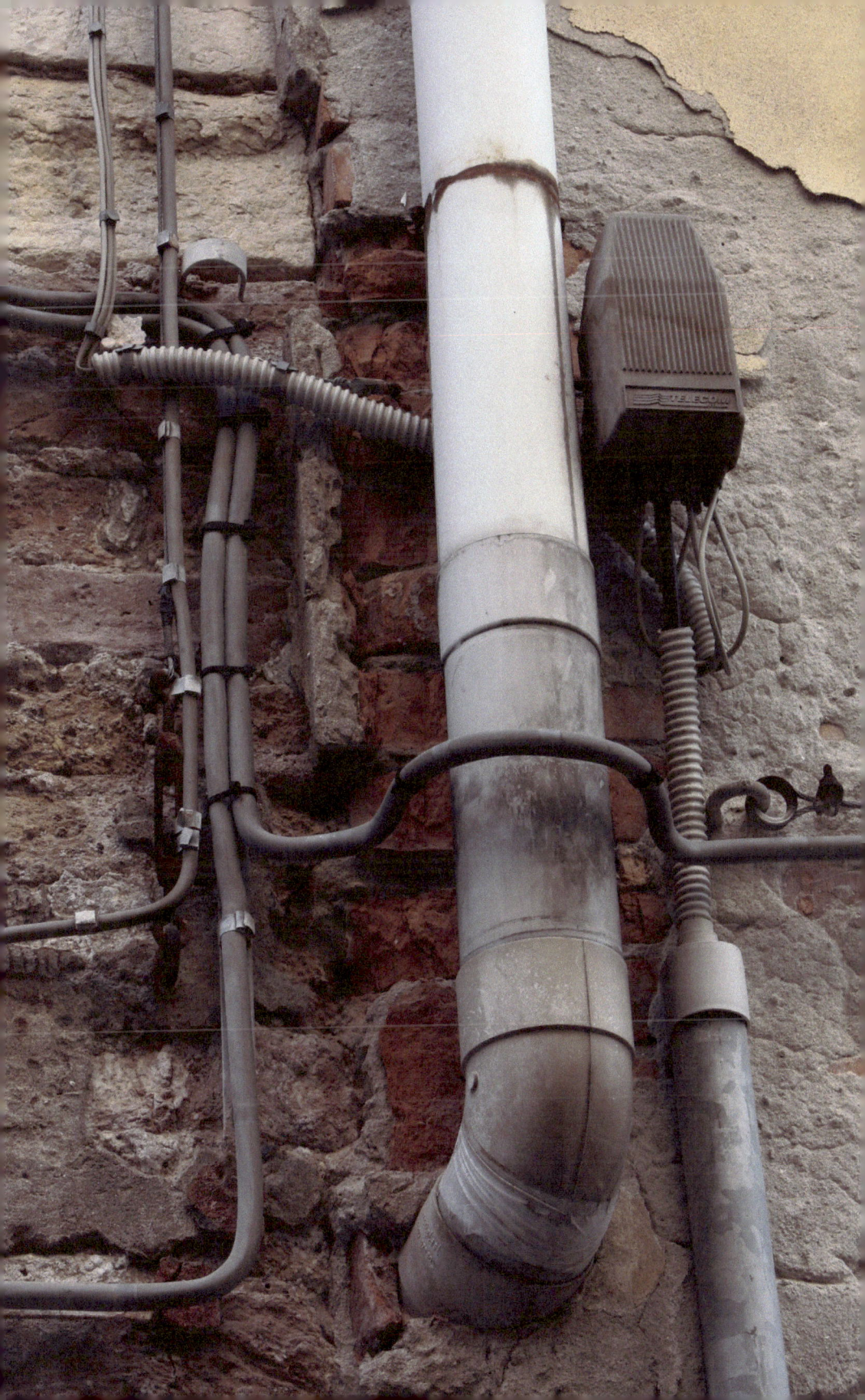

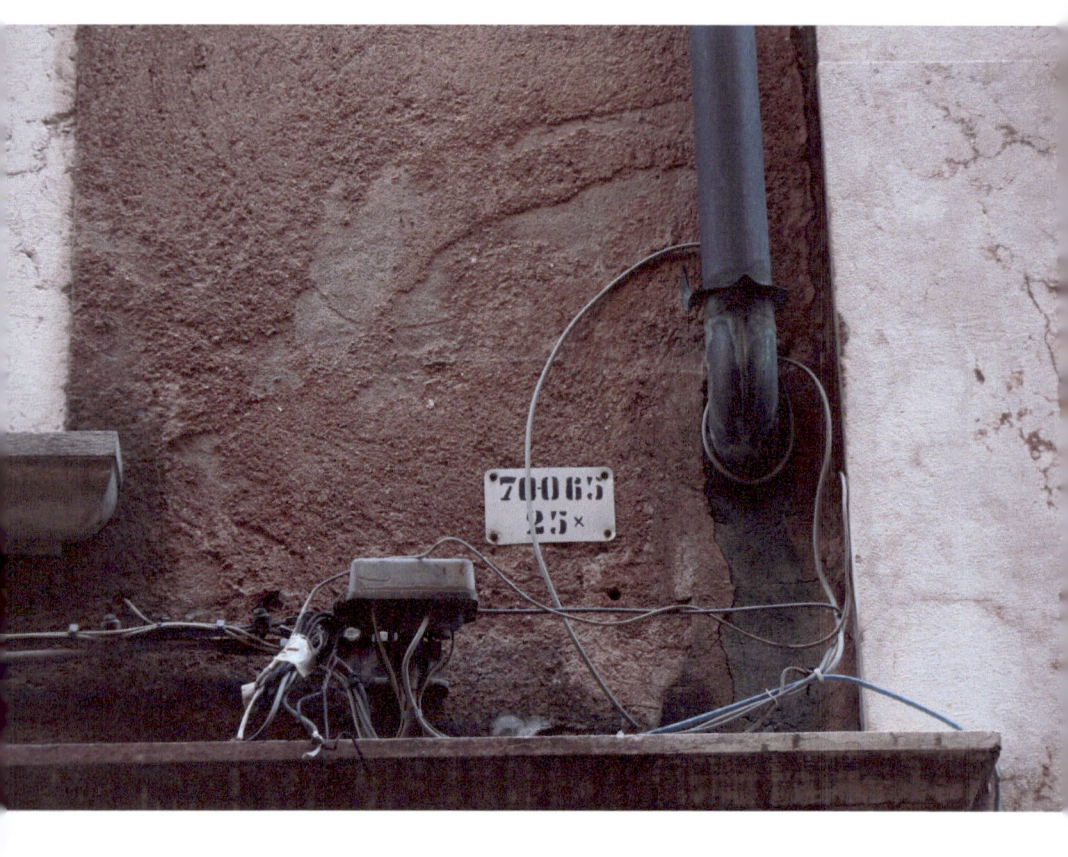

And then, to his stack,
the boy added some
of his inheritance money.

Everyone else started with $1,500.

Not the boy! Not this time!
He started with $15,000!
Ten times as much!

You might think
his friends would object.

They did not.

It was his money
to use however he wanted.

What did they care
how he used his money?

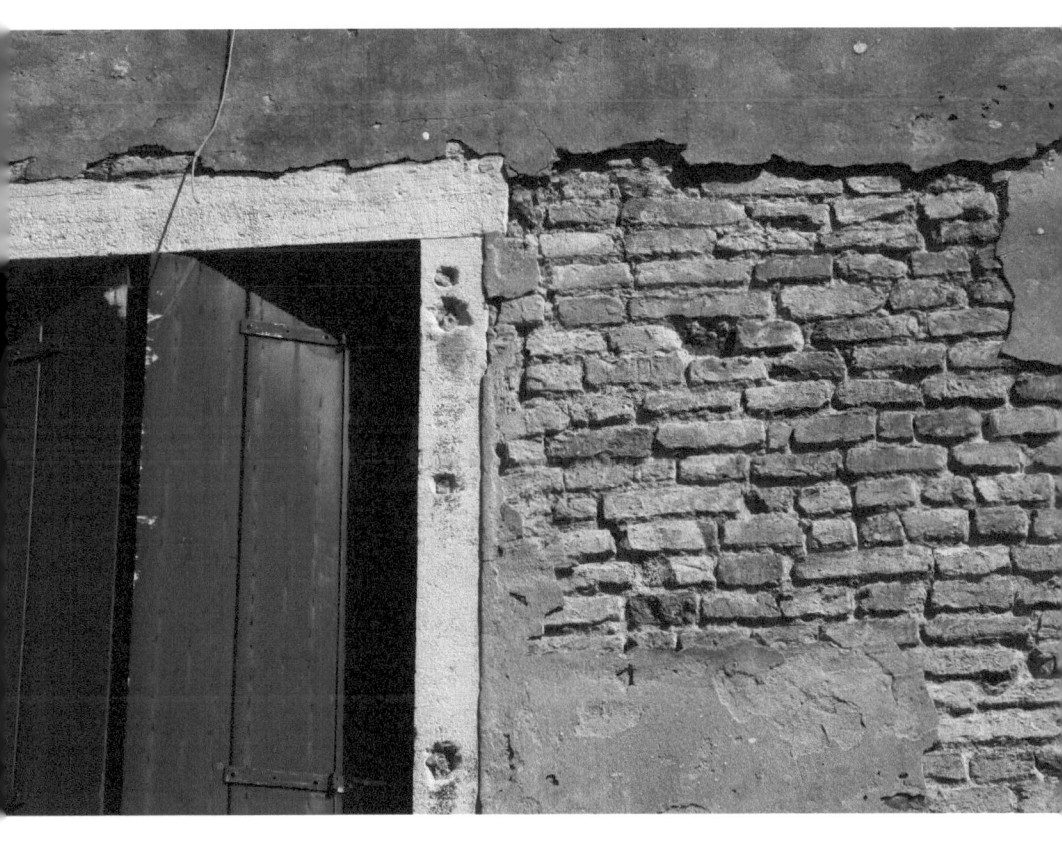

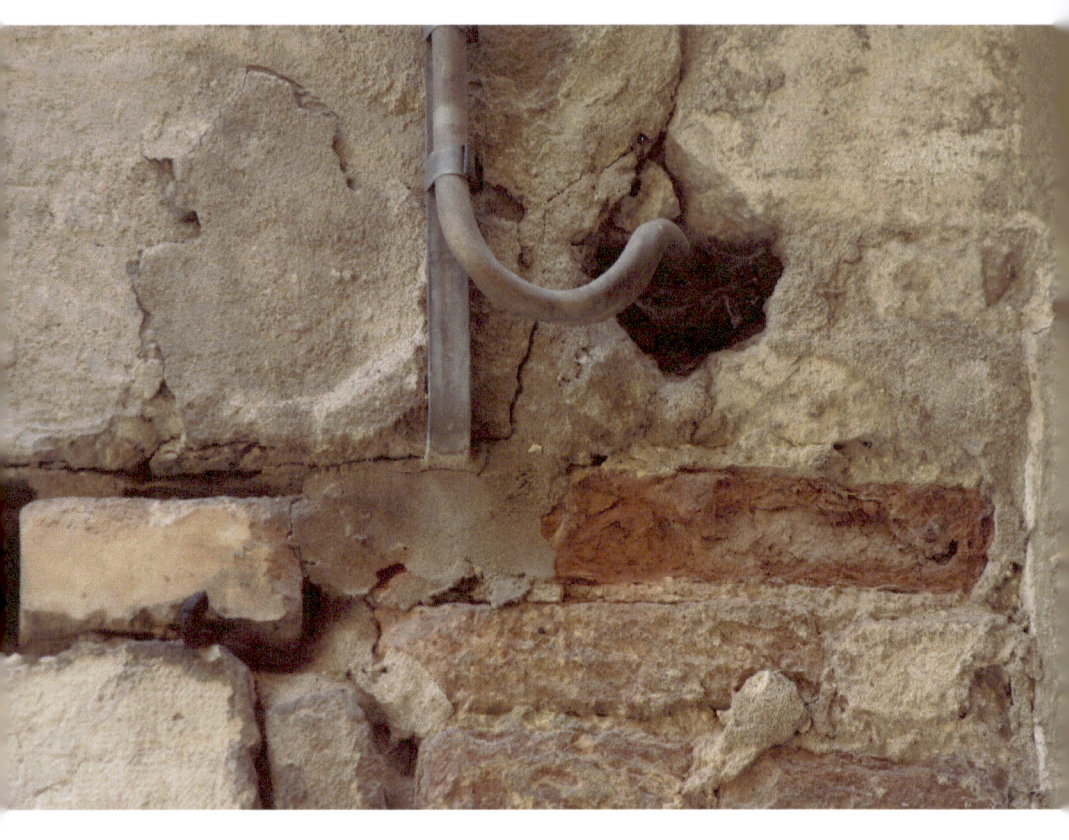

As it turned out,
the extra money
was *just* the boost
his skills needed.

He had enough money
to buy extra property
and extra houses
and extra hotels.

Soon he had
the most expensive places
on the board.

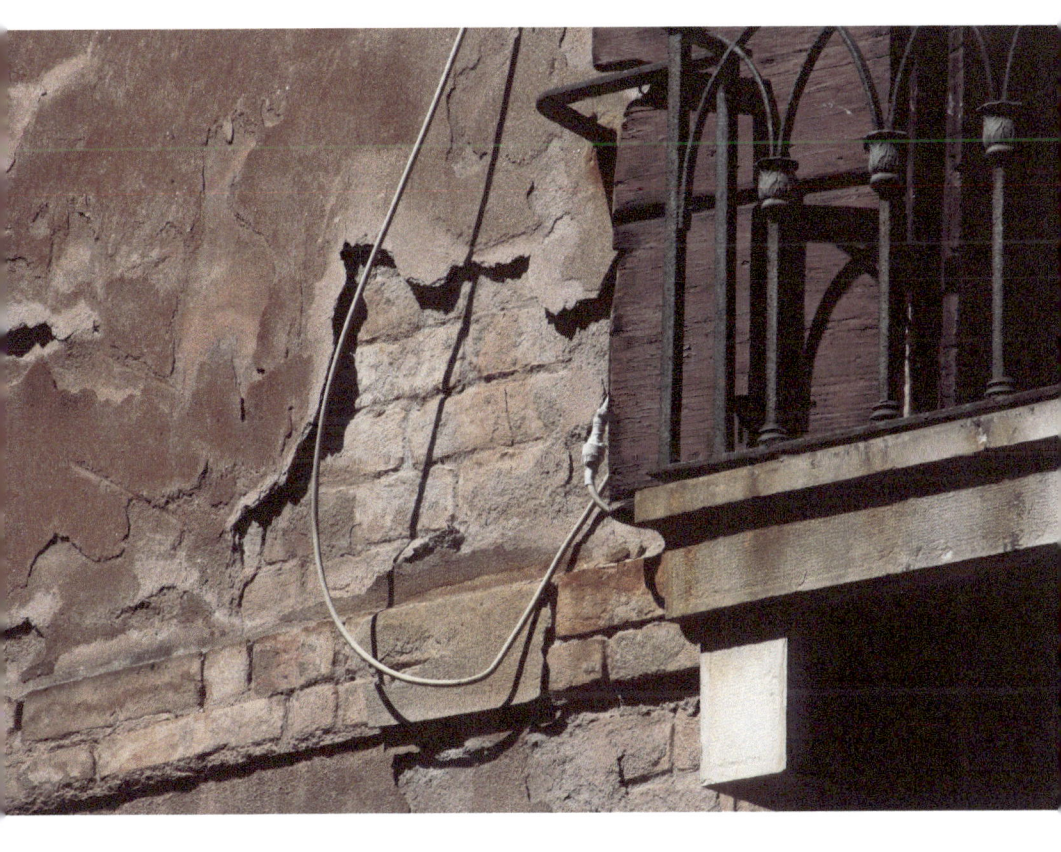

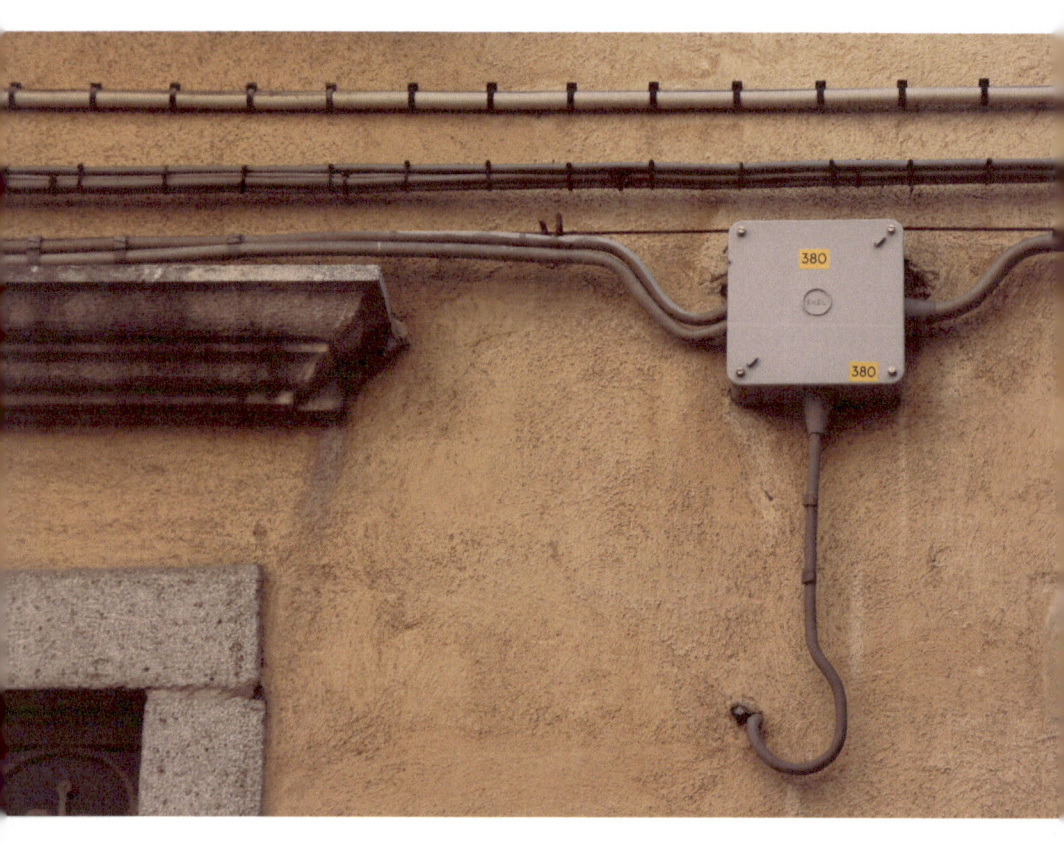

In short order
 – at least for Monopoly –
the boy won.

He was delighted.
He was *thrilled.*

He rarely won.
And this time, he'd won!

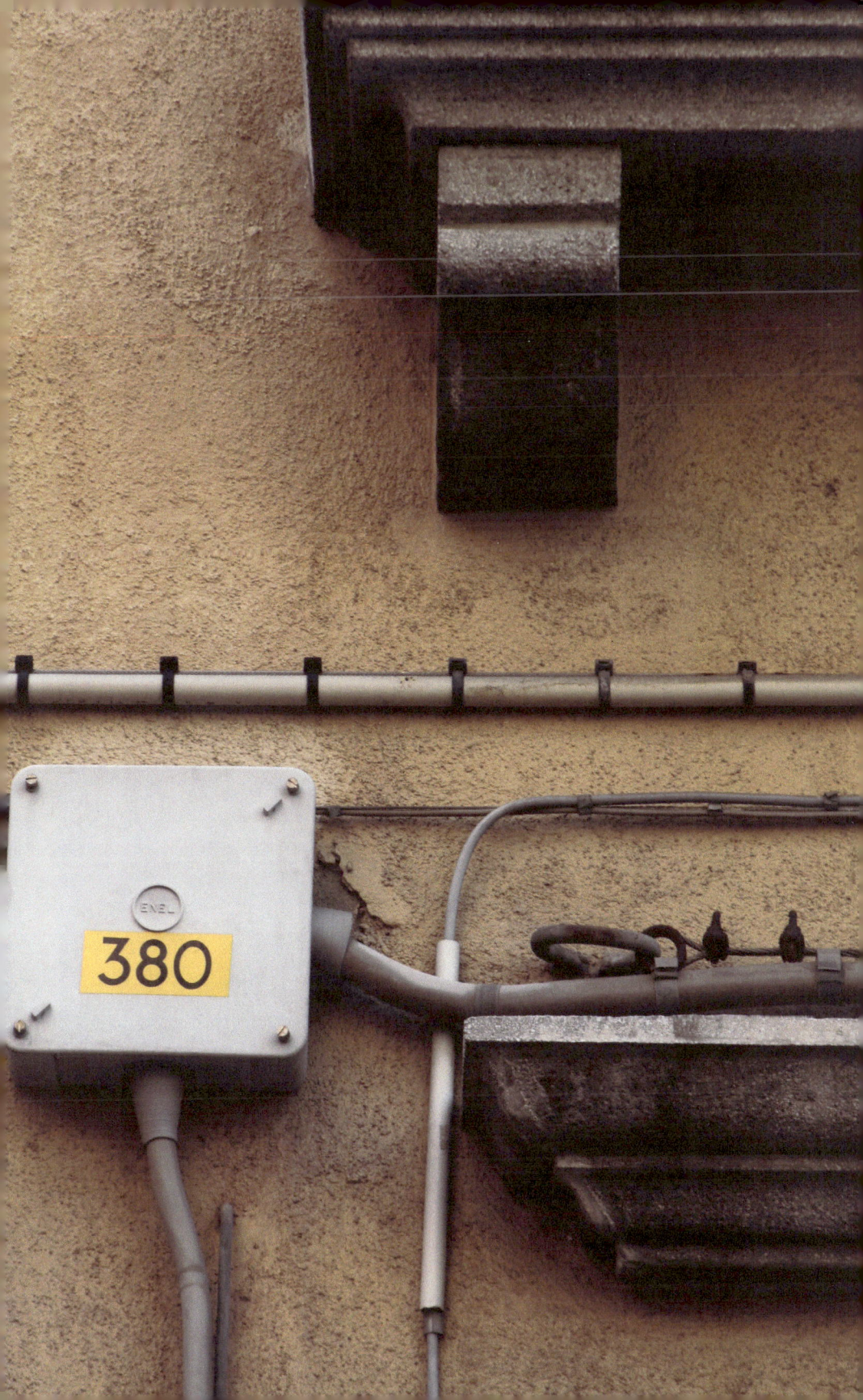

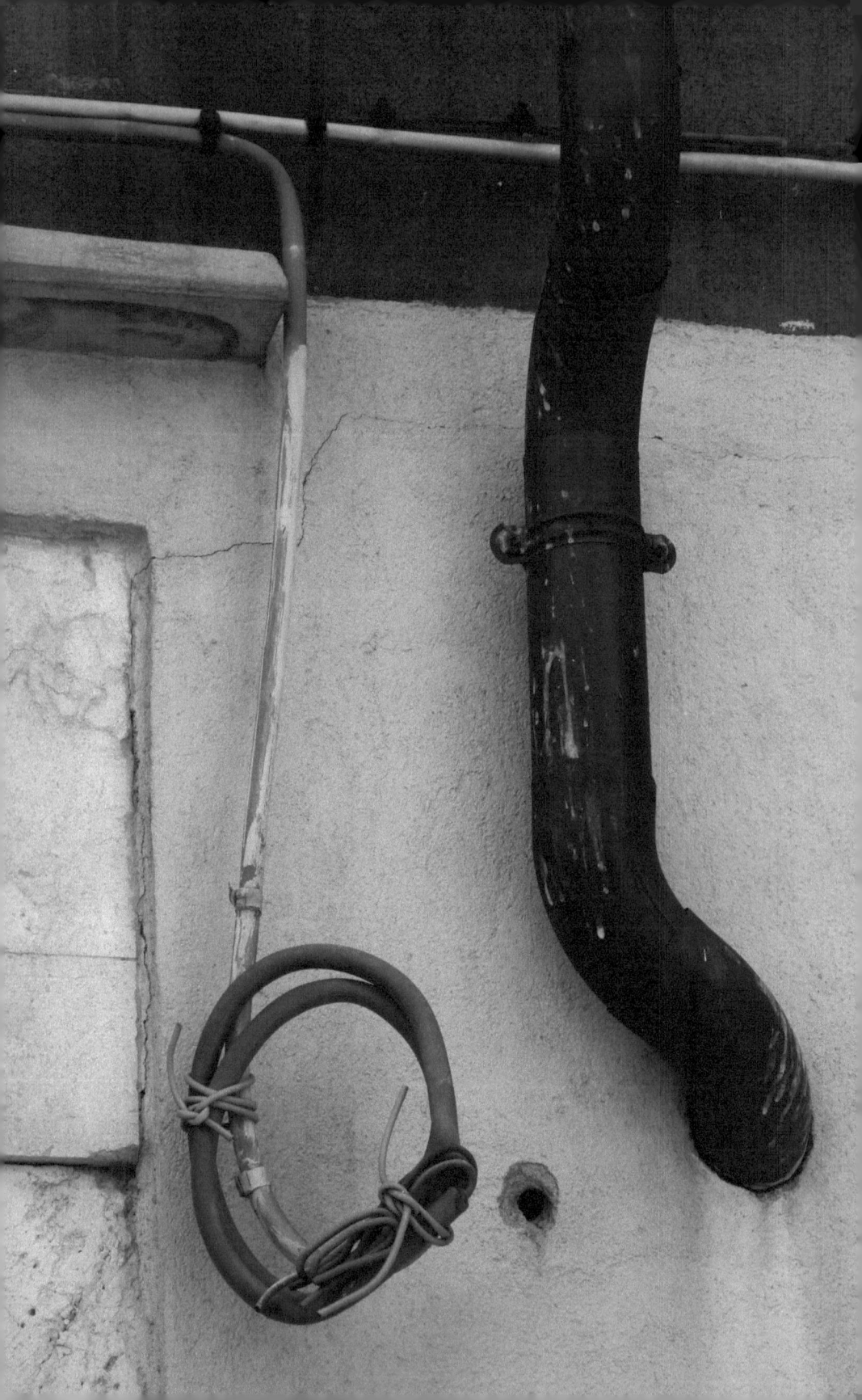

What a great day!
It was a spectacular day!
He couldn't *believe*
his good fortune!

What a wonderful inheritance!

This was one of the best things
that had ever happened to him!

He'd actually *won!*

The boy was so thrilled
he almost forgot
to help his friends
put the pieces of the game away.

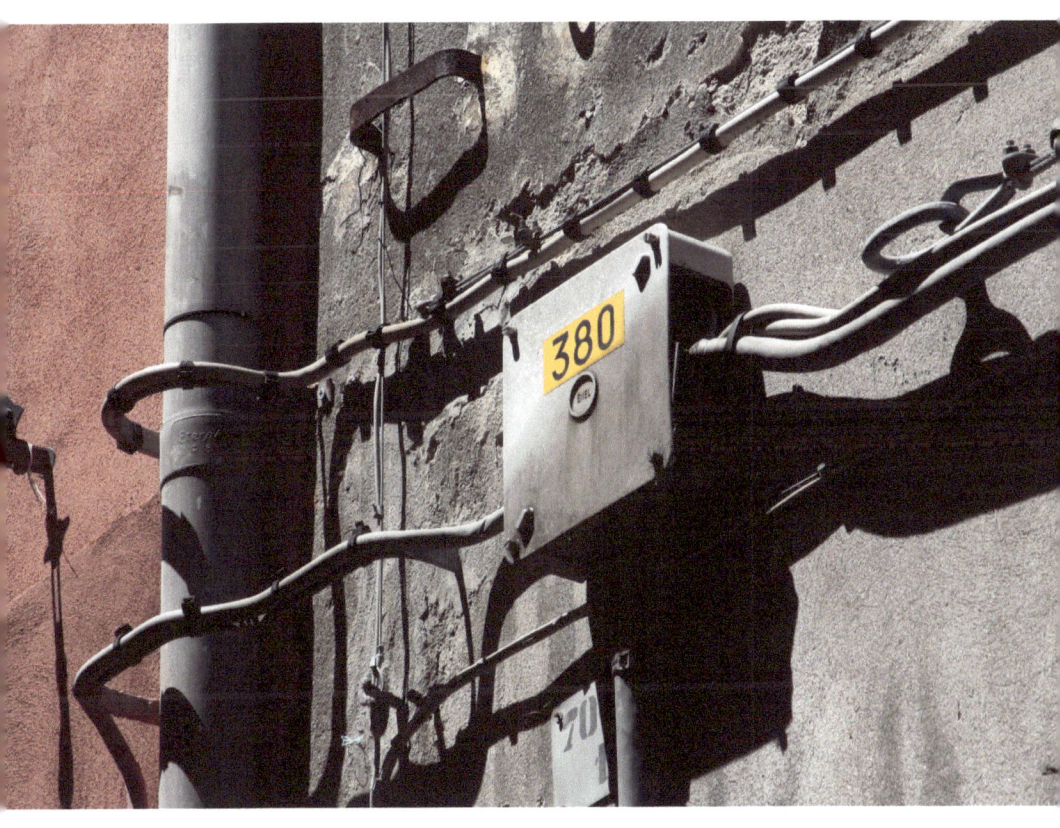

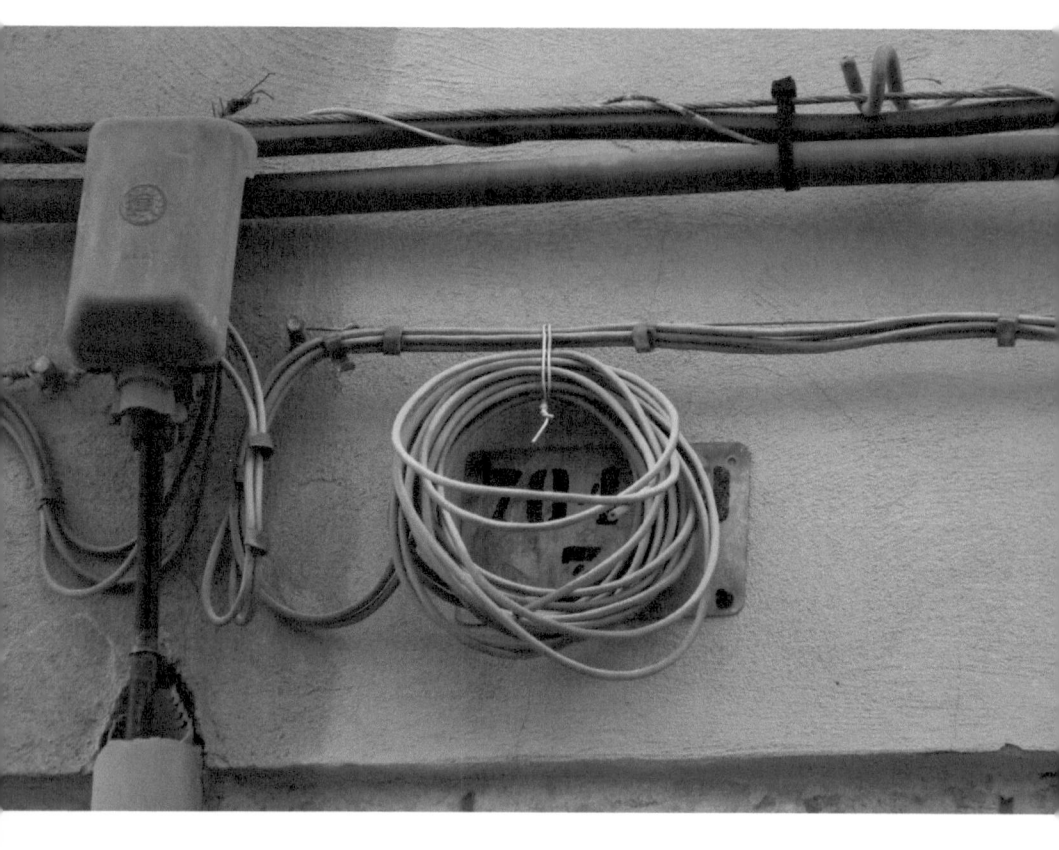

The orange Chance cards
went in one compartment.

The yellow Community Chest cards
went in another compartment.

The Scotty dog and the battleship
and the iron and the shoe
went in a third compartment.

The property deeds
went in a fourth compartment.

Then the money was put away.

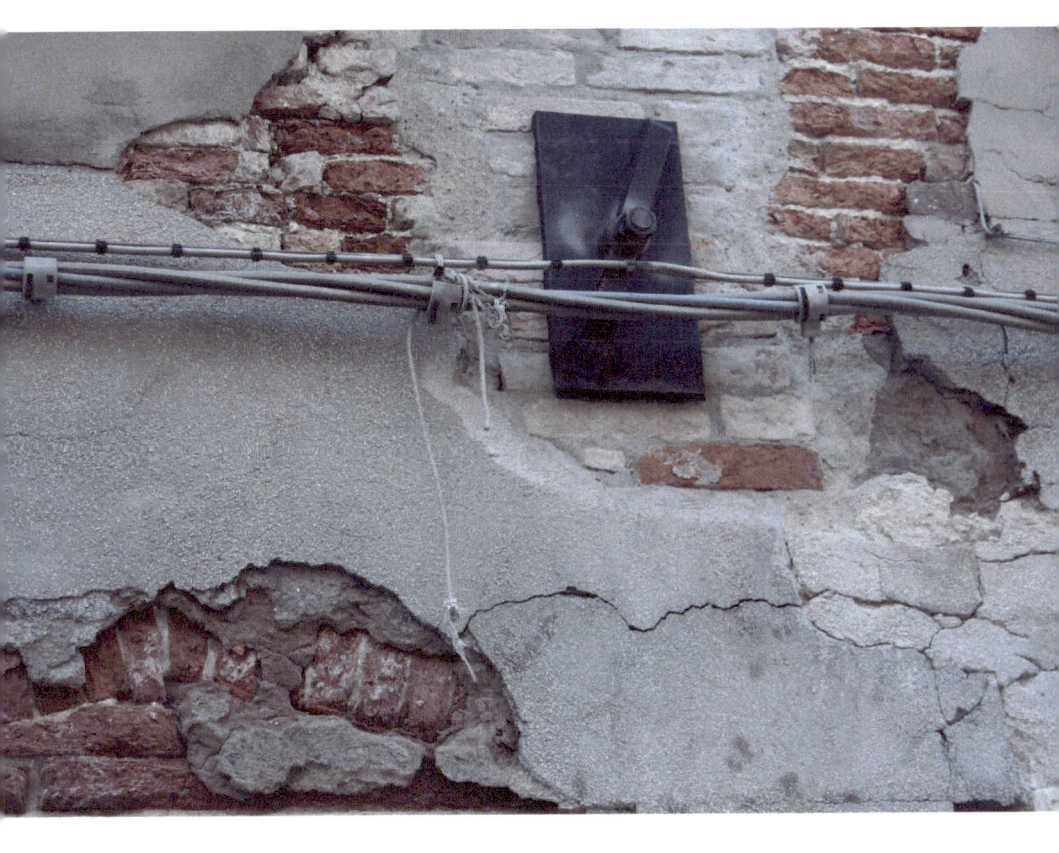

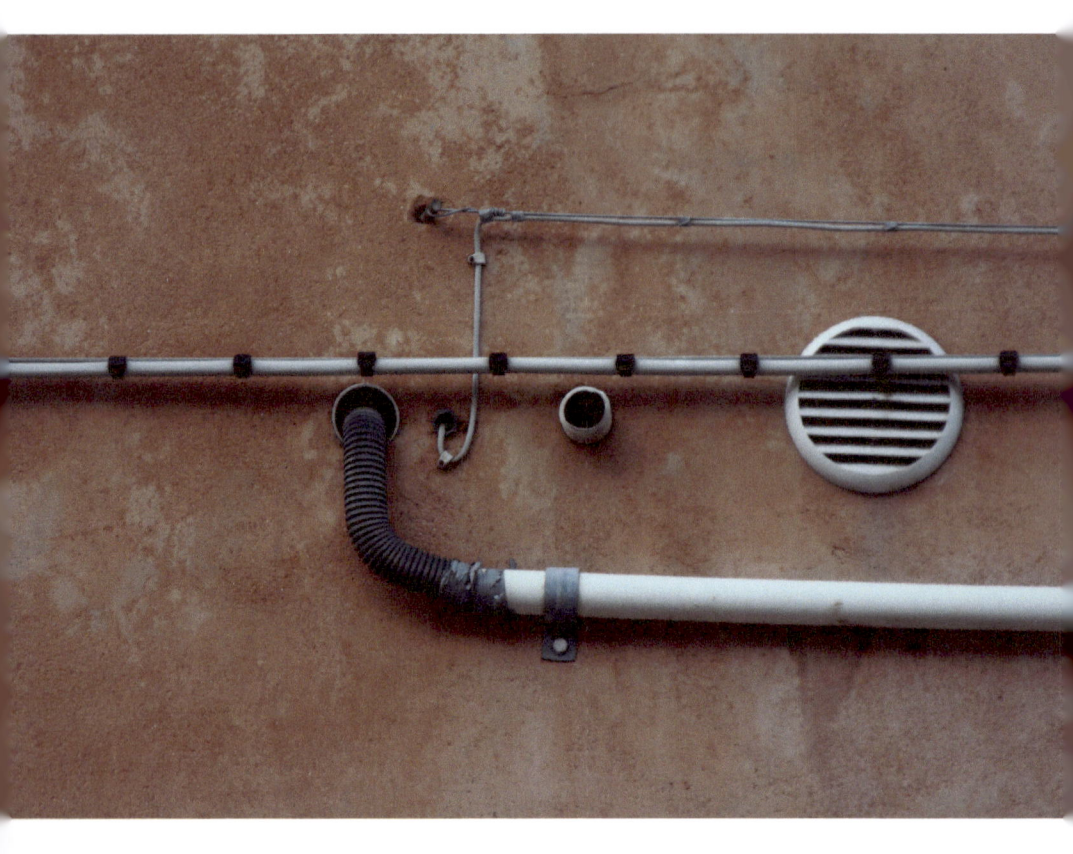

There were no extra slots
to keep the inheritance money
separate from the Monopoly money.

All the $1 bills went in the first slot.

All the $5 bills went in the second slot.

All the $10 bills went in the third slot.

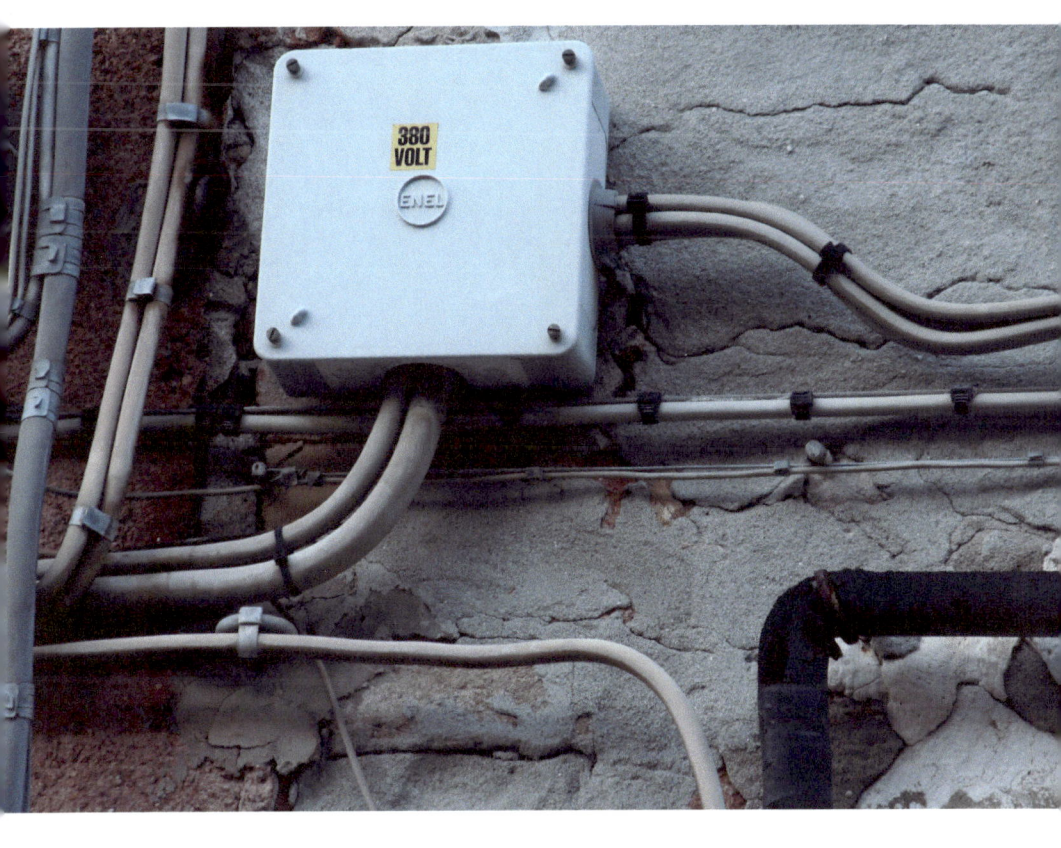

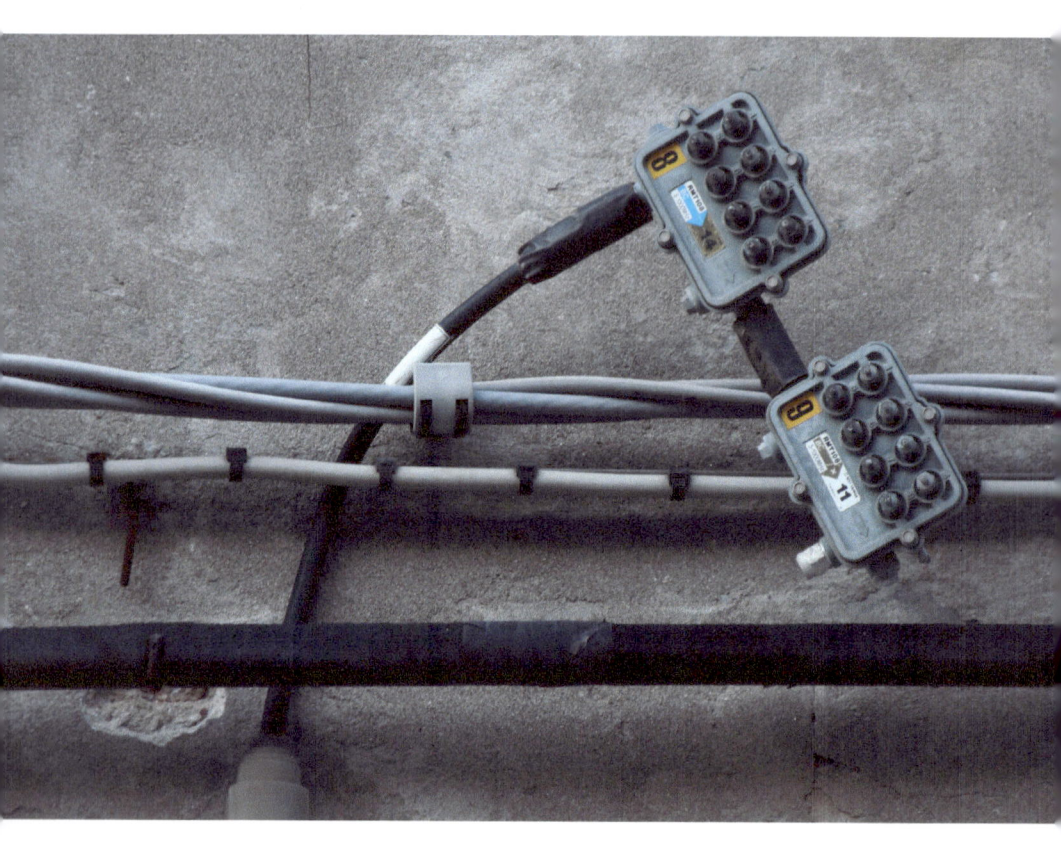

All the $20 bills went in the fourth slot.

All the $50 bills went in the fifth slot.

All the $100 bills went in the sixth slot.

All the $500 bills went in the seventh slot.

Then the playing board was folded
and put on top of the money.

The lid was put on the box.

The box was put away.

And the boy went home.

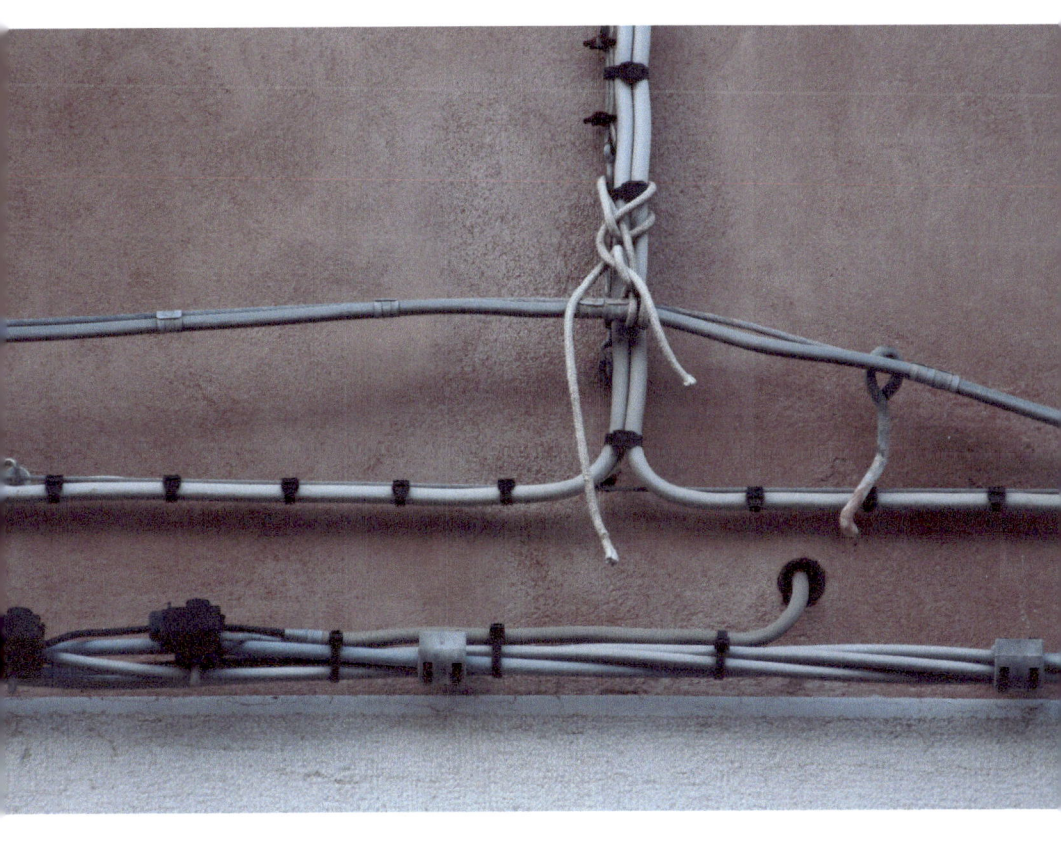

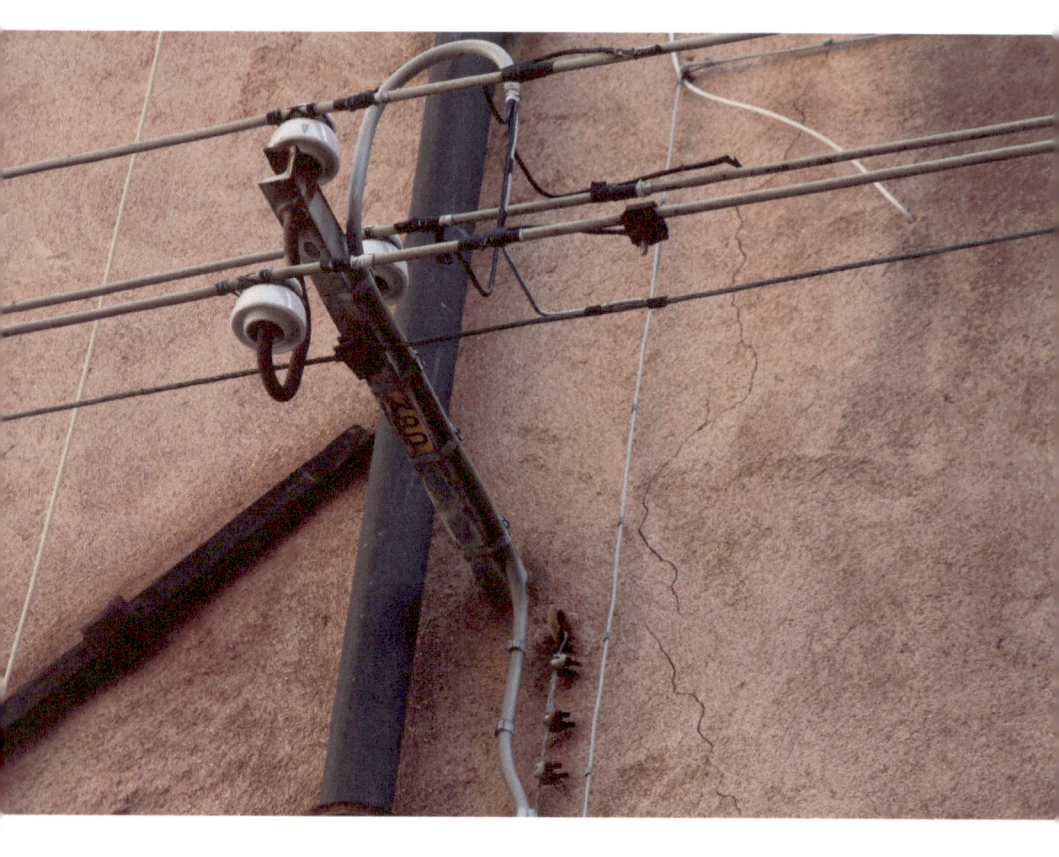

He was thrilled.
He was *beaming.*
He'd *won a game!*
What a *great* day.

He thought it might be
the *best* day of his life.

~ ~ ~

Reflection Questions

You probably haven't inherited
any money this week.

But you have lots of gifts
and lots of things that
you are good at –
or could be
after you get more practice.

What will *you* do
with all the gifts that *you* have?

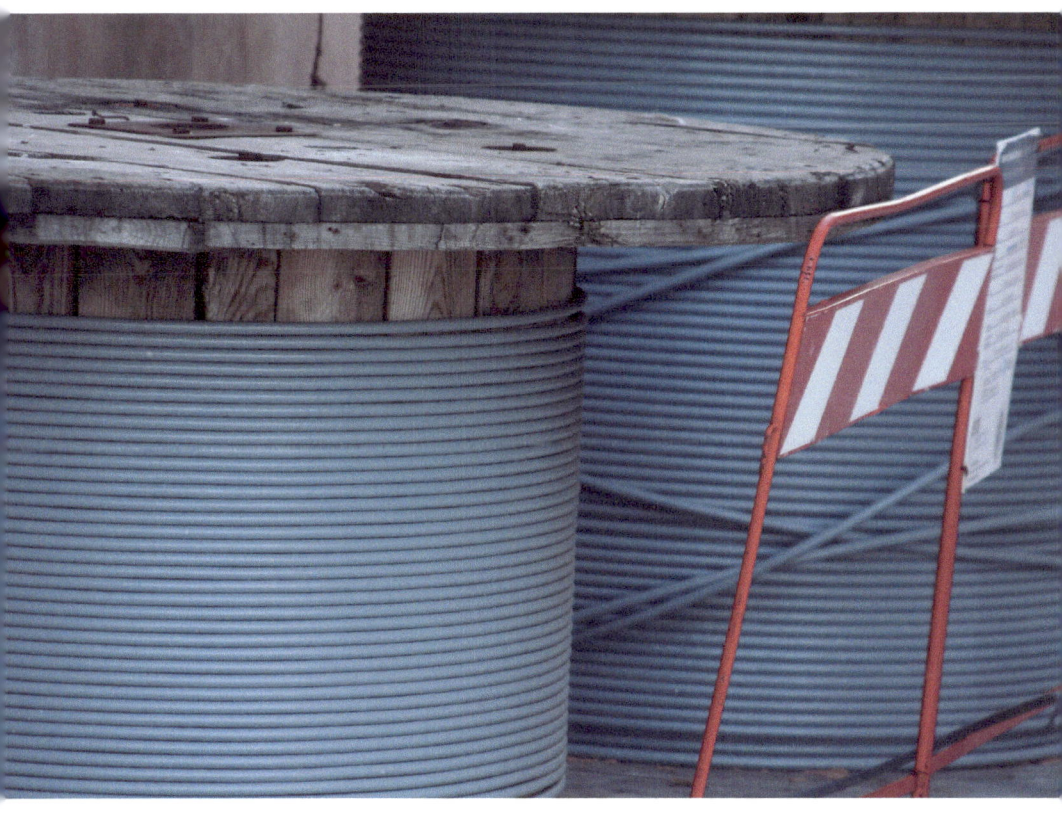

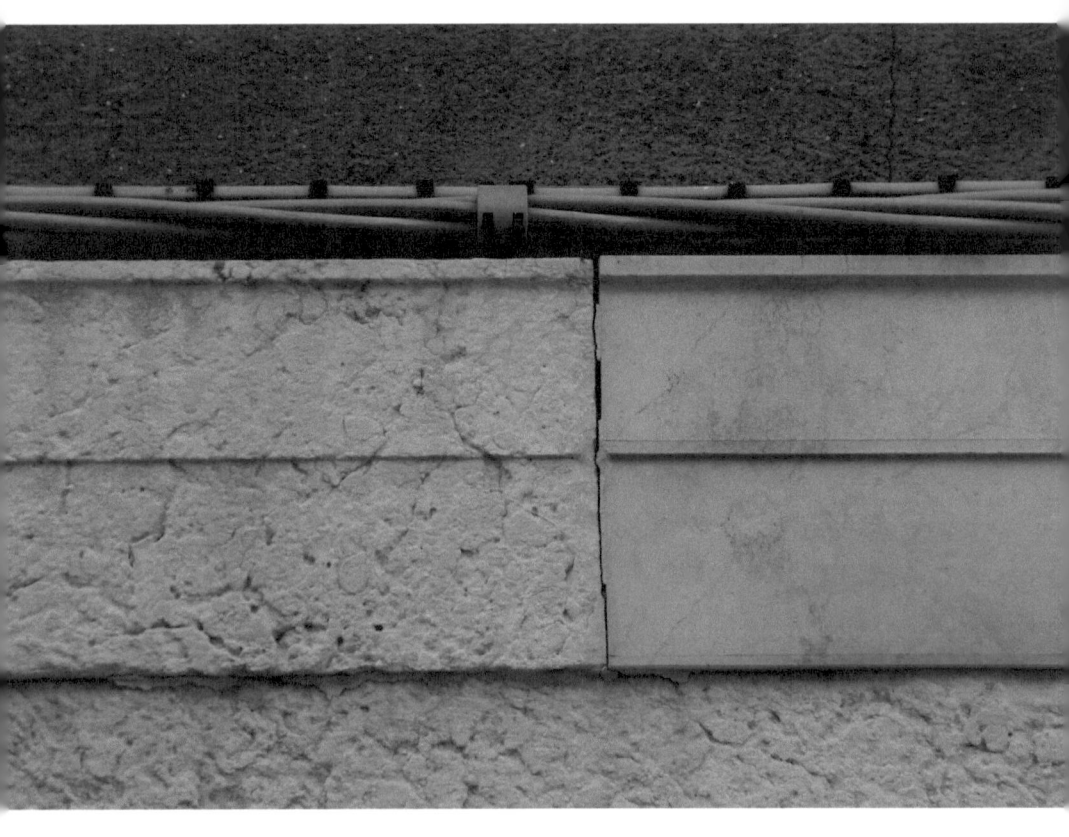

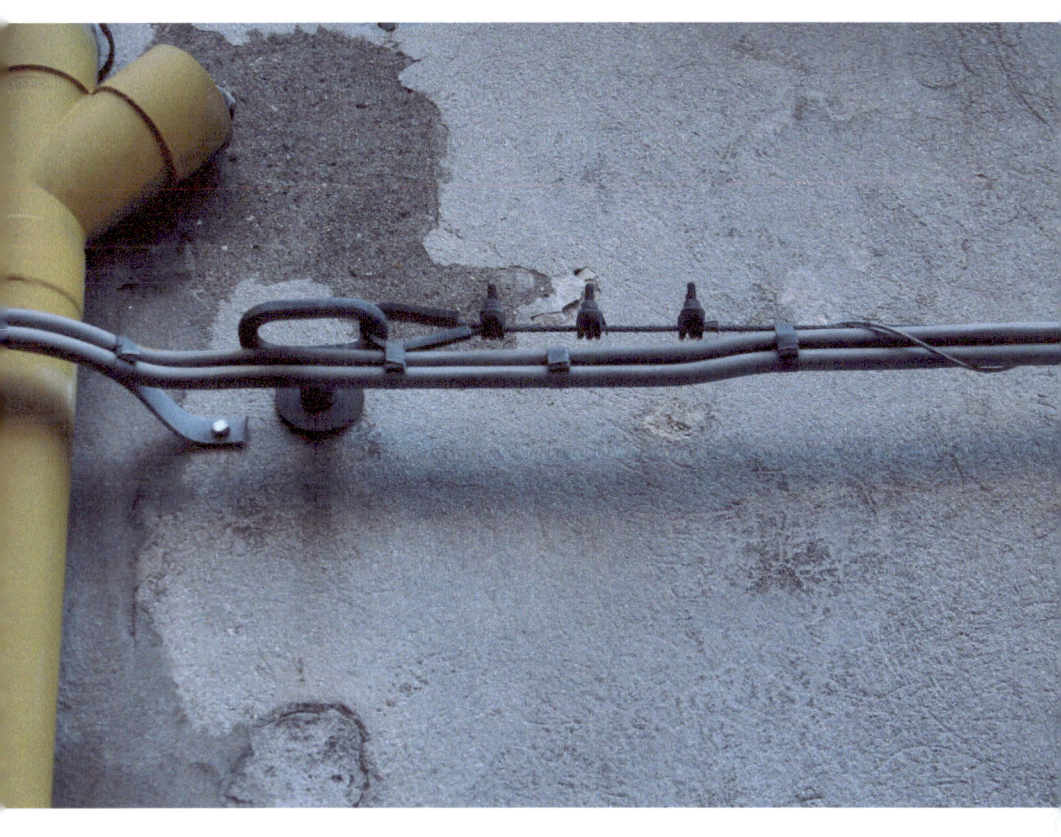

This Mark Dahle Portfolio includes a gorgeous abstract painting, twenty-five beautiful photographs of construction in Basel, Switzerland, and a story about a group of trolls moving to Norway.

When the trolls moved, they had to pass through a large forest. The trees and the trolls kept bumping into each other. It was no fault of the trees.

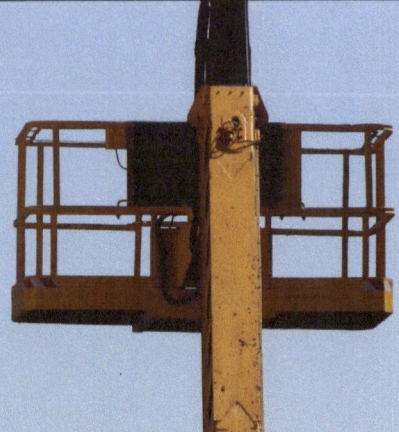

A Mark Dahle Portfolio

When The Trolls Moved

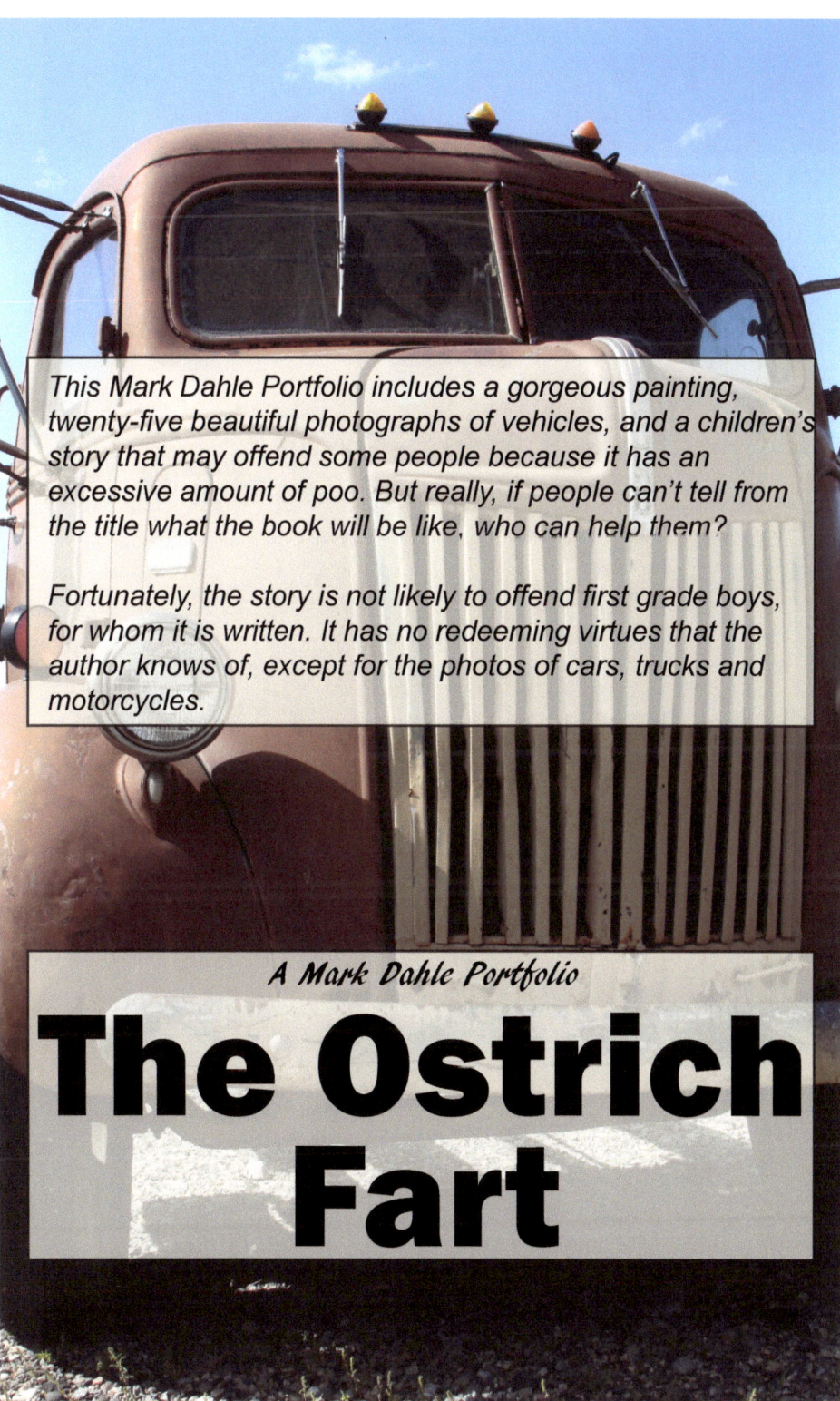

This Mark Dahle Portfolio includes a gorgeous painting, twenty-five beautiful photographs of vehicles, and a children's story that may offend some people because it has an excessive amount of poo. But really, if people can't tell from the title what the book will be like, who can help them?

Fortunately, the story is not likely to offend first grade boys, for whom it is written. It has no redeeming virtues that the author knows of, except for the photos of cars, trucks and motorcycles.

A Mark Dahle Portfolio

The Ostrich Fart

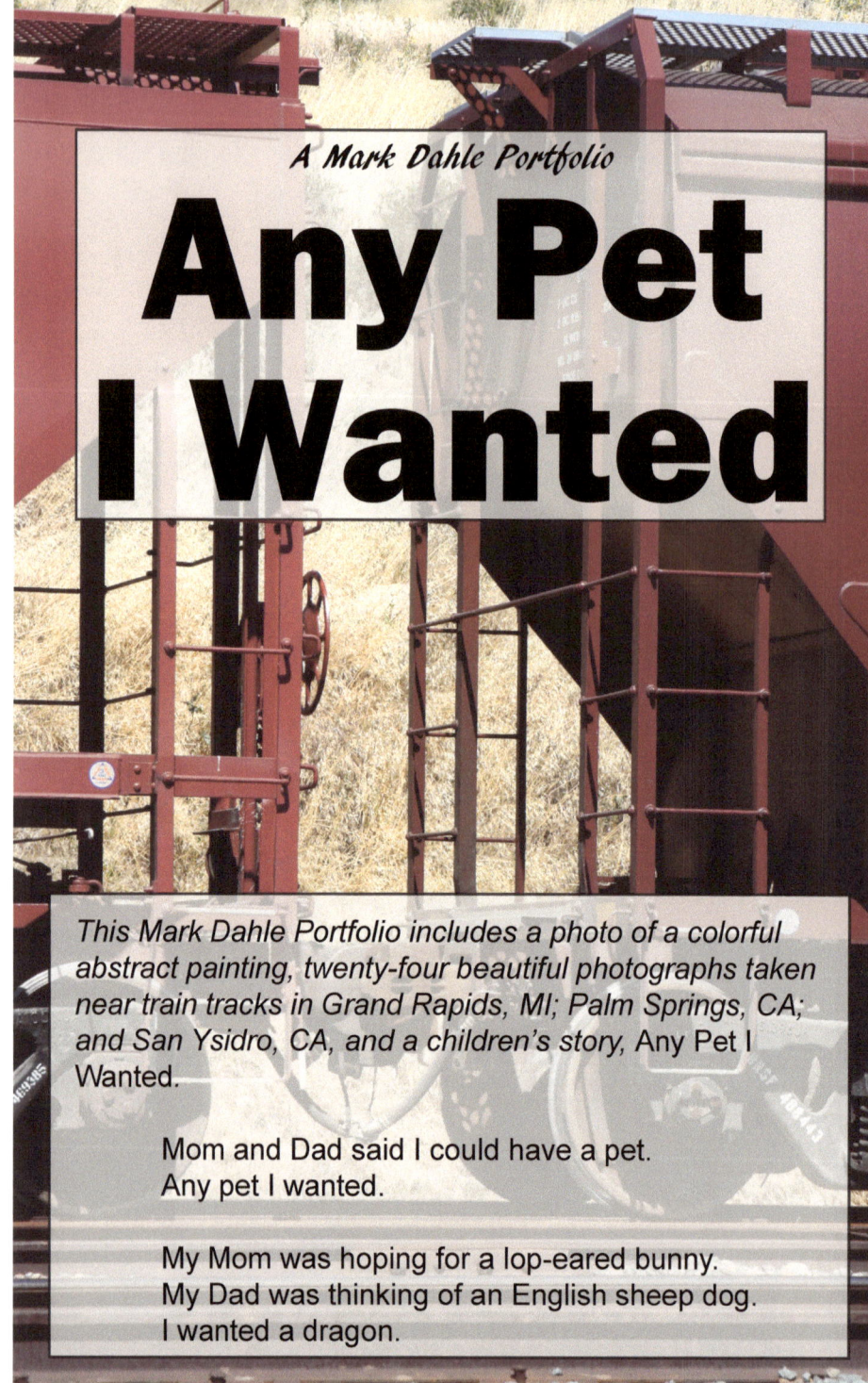

A Mark Dahle Portfolio

Any Pet
I Wanted

This Mark Dahle Portfolio includes a photo of a colorful abstract painting, twenty-four beautiful photographs taken near train tracks in Grand Rapids, MI; Palm Springs, CA; and San Ysidro, CA, and a children's story, Any Pet I Wanted.

Mom and Dad said I could have a pet.
Any pet I wanted.

My Mom was hoping for a lop-eared bunny.
My Dad was thinking of an English sheep dog.
I wanted a dragon.

www.ingramcontent.com/pod-product-compliance
Lightning Source LLC
Chambersburg PA
CBHW040857180526
45159CB00001B/443